SAFE AND PR(
SHORT TERM AND HO

A complete guide for property owners

Mi Casa Su Casa Consulting
October 2015

ISBN 978-1518715624

First Edition 2015

For new projects or enquiries related to the topics discussed in this book you can contact us at enquiries@micasasucasa-consulting.com

Disclaimer
Although the author and publisher have made every effort to ensure that the information in this book was correct at press time, the author and publisher do not assume and hereby disclaim any liability to any party for any loss, damage, or disruption caused by errors or omissions, whether such errors or omissions result from negligence, accident, or any other cause.

Table of Contents

1 Introduction

The topic of short term or holiday letting is becoming more and more popular all over the world, and with good reason. For the vast majority of people, their house is the largest investment and it remains the biggest financial burden until the mortgage is paid back many years later.

At the same time, even primary residences can be vacant at various times of the year such as when owners go on business trips or holidays.

On the other side of the accommodation spectrum, the tourism and travel industry is changing all over the world. Larger families and groups of friends find hotels and serviced apartments inadequate for their needs and search for larger, better equipped and more community-friendly solutions.

The natural synergies between the above three vectors create an ideal business opportunity for property owners everywhere.

As an active professional in this new industry, I have spent the last years of my long hospitality career building and implementing business models for property owners. This in-depth knowledge and constant contact with owners and travellers has helped me to discover the significance of a fourth and essential element - the emotional involvement that every owner must understand before embarking on this new and lucrative enterprise.

If the first three components can be quantified and then used in forecasts and business plans, adding the emotional element to the mix requires a careful and holistic look at the entire process of letting the property out. In the final chapter of this book, I take an in-depth look at this matter and try to help the reader assess how likely it is that this business will be an enjoyable effort.

While the business idea is quite straightforward, its successful implementation is a different story. There are many reasons for this but none more significant than the wide range of skills needed to create the guest experience cycle. Think of setting expectations during the marketing stage, managing payments, damage cover guarantees and refunds, preparing accurate inventories pre and post-stay, arranging the meet and greet, repairing the odd boiler within the expected timeframe or troubleshooting faulty keys or broken windows. They are all part of the job as a host and involve different sets of skills.

This guidebook is based on my personal experience in advising and delivering this service to thousands of owners and guests in London, United Kingdom, and is also adapted for many international markets where the same business model is rapidly taking shape. Aside from certain legal differences, the model is very similar and can be applied successfully to any destination in the world. With this goal in mind, and because I wanted to make this guide as time-proof as possible, I didn't include the usual links to the hot-shot companies of the day but rather trained the reader in how to find the most actual and relevant providers at the time of reading the book.

In my advisory role I was in charge of creating the standards for service delivery for both the hosts and their guests, and this has given me a unique view on the needs, expectations and the successful strategy needed for this business model.

My advice is the result of years of creating, testing, amending, adapting and constantly listening to the feedback received from all stakeholders. To the best of my knowledge, this is the first in-depth effort to organise the information about this new business model in an efficient and realistic way which can be applied immediately for a safe and profitable business initiative.

The material is organised into a workbook format with checklists at the end of each chapter and will be of great help to anyone interested in the field. Complete beginners can follow the process step-by-step while more experienced operators may want to review their processes and align them to what I consider to be a very solid blueprint for service delivery excellence.

Much effort and passion went into creating this book and I hope that the knowledge I am sharing will add real value to the lives of all the hosts and their guests around the world.

Chapter checklist

✓ Are you comfortable with the idea of giving access to your property to complete strangers?

✓ Are you permitted to rent out or sub-let your property from a legal point of view?

✓ Are all co-owners (if applicable) in agreement about this business venture?

✓ Is your entire house available for rent for at least one week every year?

If the answer is 'yes' to all of the above, read on and get ready for an exciting business opportunity!

2 Legislation and tax

The most important aspect to remember is that legislation is not consistent and even neighbouring councils may regulate the activity differently. However, as this new industry matures, this will change and more uniform regulation may be introduced, although the rule of thumb is to check the current legislation with your local authority. I strongly recommend careful research before setting up your business or enlisting the help of an accountant or legal representative. The following paragraphs are just for guidance and support during the initial stage of research and are not to be considered as legal advice.

However fragmented the legal framework around the world, the following areas must be considered, regardless of the current situation. It may look daunting at first but the process is often quite quick and simple.

- ✓ Local authority regulations
- ✓ Leasehold agreement for subletting (if renting and not owning)
- ✓ Mortgage (and loans secured on it) clauses related to renting
- ✓ Property Insurance
- ✓ Public Liability Insurance
- ✓ Income Tax
- ✓ Fire, Gas and Electrical Equipment safety check certificates
- ✓ Health & Safety regulations for general trips and falls
- ✓ Property Description regulations

The concept of short term and holiday rentals is taking the world by storm and more and more people are realising its potential. The challenge is to adapt the laws and regulations to reflect these realities and to contribute to a better outcome for all stakeholders.

This is easier said than done however due to the financial and social implications of accepting holiday rentals as part of the new travel industry. The 'sharing' economy has exploded almost everywhere in the world and companies such as Airbnb®, HomeAway® or FlipKey® are at the forefront of an important effort to change the travel paradigms and usher in a new business model. Their example has been followed by many other start-ups around the world.

My observation is that there is still resistance in the marketplace and there are a number of players with vested interests, but the most influential by far are the hotel and serviced apartments businesses as well as the local councils. On the one hand, the new model has the potential to steal market share from the traditional lodging solutions and put a lot more pressure on the long term residential rental market, while on the other hand, local councils warn that unregulated activity can lead to disturbances and bad practices in highly sought after residential areas. Also, an increase in short term letting can contribute to further housing problems in busy metropolitan areas as landlords will shift availability to this new distribution channel.

This state of affairs is reflected in the way that the local councils approach the new demand and the reality is that regulations are constantly changing and that precedent does not always guarantee that other local authorities will vote for change.

Reporting and collecting income tax in relation to the short term rental industry is also a big topic and, as one would expect, a key driver in the decision making process. That is why it is essential to take advice on tax matters before anything else.

However, all of the above concerns fail to take into account the fact that the world is changing and the travel industry could benefit greatly from this extremely vast pool of international accommodation resources. Property owners in many cities around the world are starting to join professional associations created with the goal of protecting the interests of those in the short term rental industry.

The examples below from around the world show how fragmented the legislation is. The following commentaries are relevant at the time of writing this book and may change. As suggested in the first paragraph of this chapter, before starting out it is essential to obtain the most recent set of laws regulating this activity as this chapter is just initial guidance and not specialised legal advice.

London

In England, and London in particular, it is now permissible to rent your property out for up to 90 days a year without having to apply for planning permission. Until very recently, this wasn't the case, and property owners could face fines of up to £20,000 for renting out without formal approval from local councils.

However, this doesn't mean that there is no more resistance, as some councils have already declared their intentions to prepare proposals for a reduction from 90 days to a maximum of 30 days.

Northern Ireland

In Northern Ireland, currently all tourist accommodation activities must be authorised and issued with a special certificate.

San Francisco

San Francisco is one of the first cities in the world to make short term rentals legal. Although recently the municipality passed a law allowing short term rentals for up to 90 days a year, there is already pressure from housing and other hospitality supporters to introduce amendments to the law to limit this cap or impose further controls.

New York City

As one would expect, New York City is one of the most active players in the short term lettings industry, yet the current state and local laws prohibit this activity for the vast majority of the properties there. The regulations apply to all stays of 30 days or less and even if there are differences between Class A and Class B multiple dwelling units, there is overlap with other laws so that renting out is either completely prohibited or very limited for un-hosted units.

Santa Monica

The city of Santa Monica completely barred all types of short term rentals for full units, while the authorities in Los Angeles are trying to curb and regulate the illegal short term rentals which were left unchecked for quite a while in recent years. According to the current zoning laws, almost all short term rentals are illegal.

Paris

In Paris, the situation is different again. Under French law, the owners are allowed to rent out to short term guests as long as they do this from their primary residence. Although the law requires owners to report and register, this rarely happens and the municipality is now looking for ways to crack down on these practices to the detriment of the new short term rentals industry. New amendments introduce financial commitments and obligations for property owners, making this more expensive and difficult to be put in practice by owners with only one unit to rent.

Madrid and Barcelona

Spain displays a different kind of regulatory landscape. While all 17 Autonomous Communities have taken an active role in regulating this practice, there are still differences when it comes to the length of stay and the standards to be observed. Although in many Communities (but not all), it is legal to let the property for short term stays, the owner must register with the local authority and comply with a comprehensive list of standards for the provision of internet access, air conditioning and ventilation, first aid kits, certain furniture and even local guide books. With regard to the minimum length of stay, the legislation in Madrid still prohibits rentals for less than five days for primary residences.

At the time of writing the book, this article was coming under pressure and there was hope that the minimum duration would be dropped. Overall, even if the law seems more permissive here compared to other countries, the regional diversity invites caution and I suggest that interested landlords take legal advice to ensure that they are on the right side of the law and to avoid hefty fines. Barcelona has a long history of resisting short term rentals and recently even applied big fines to companies in the sector.

Amsterdam

Amsterdam is a much friendlier destination. The law allows short term rentals for up to two months a year, with up to four people at a time in a rental unit. However, the landlords must register with the local authorities and pay a tourist tax on top of the relevant taxes.

Munich, Berlin, Hamburg

In Germany, the local authorities in cities like Munich, Berlin or Hamburg have introduced laws to crack down on short term holiday rentals. It is now a legal requirement to register and apply for permission before renting out a property and special inspectors go around the central neighbourhoods to check that the laws are respected.

Greek Islands

In Greece, all holiday rentals must be licenced by the Greek Tourist Organisation (EOT). There is a very comprehensive set of requirements and the government regulations ensure that legal operators comply with all standards of Health & Safety and comfort. It is worth mentioning that the licensing process also checks the owner's criminal and tax records.

Tokyo and Osaka

Japan has great potential for the sharing economy but currently, landlords cannot rent out without a special licence and very specific requirements for room size and services. However, it has been announced that due to severe shortages in the accommodation capacity, authorities in Osaka may consider relaxing the law.

Australia

In Australia, there is a lot of confusion and hesitation when it comes to this topic. Although homeowners in Victoria and Queensland benefit from clearer legislation compared to NSW, they still need to seek advice from the local councils. Until broader reaching changes are introduced, it appears that this activity will continue to be assessed on a case-by-case basis.

Canada

Although Canada is known for its relaxed approach to the sharing economy, there are already signs that local provinces will soon start regulating the short term rental market. Quebec is the first to have gone down this road and this will surely bring further obligations with which to comply with if an individual wanted to rent their property out.

The authorities in Ontario do not currently plan to regulate this market and municipalities have been granted broad powers to regulate this business in a variety of ways. In Toronto, the local authorities have conducted several internal discussions on this topic but there is no intention to take action in any way so far. The biggest concern is for owners in condominium buildings where the administrators can shut down an operation if they prove that security and order have been compromised.

South Africa

Moving to South Africa, we find a much more permissive approach to renting out short term. The most significant development in this country is the introduction of certain amendments to the Rental Housing Act, with the intention of increasing the number of written contracts for all rentals.

Sweden

Moving on again, very strict rental laws have created a host of controversy in Sweden. Residents with a contract directly with the owner of the property are allowed to sub-let the unit only under very specific circumstances, for instance when going away for a while to study, or when a partner moves in to share the property.

Even so, the owner of the property or the tenant association must sign off any such agreement. For direct owners of condominiums, the law is less clear and although some buildings allow owners to rent their property out short term, in every case the names of the guests must be registered and submitted to the housing boards in advance.

Russia

During the past few years, there have been efforts to bring the short term rentals industry to the Russian market. There is undoubtedly a massive opportunity there and the biggest challenges are more of a cultural character than anything. The most important one is trust, and although demand outstrips supply, there is still a long way to go until market participants will be comfortable in accepting card payments, booking and paying without a viewing first or giving complete strangers access to the property.

Hong Kong

Moving to the South, according to Hong Kong law, any place rented for less than 28 days requires a special hotel licence. Much is to be said about the government's ability and current interest in enforcing this law, but property owners must be aware of it. Also, if the unit is not owned but rented then the tenants must check if the contract allows sub-letting.

Mainland China

In mainland China, the regulations governing short term rentals are in a grey area and the authorities still need to provide clear instructions on taxes, safety, information dissemination and other related aspects. Demand is growing rapidly though and thanks to the large amount of properties available, the future looks bright for this location.

Dubai

Dubai benefits from very clear laws for short term and holiday rentals. All operators must obtain a special licence from the Department of Tourism and Commerce Marketing and offenders may face hefty fines. The authorities have a long term strategy of increasing accommodation capacity and this will only help this emerging industry.

It is obvious that the above analysis is not exhaustive, but highly representative for the fragmentation existent in the market. Authorities everywhere are trying to adapt to the emerging sharing economy and to balance the interests of all stakeholders but they do this with varying degrees of success. There is a constant "tug of war" between parties and this is expected to continue. That is why it is best to do your homework, take advice from the local authorities and even enlist the help of legal and tax advisors.

Chapter Checklist

✓ Local authority regulations
✓ Leasehold agreement for subletting if renting and not owning
✓ Mortgage (and loans secured on it) clauses related to renting
✓ Property Insurance
✓ Public Liability Insurance
✓ Income Tax

- ✓ Fire, Gas and Electrical Equipment safety check certificates
- ✓ Health & Safety regulations for general trips and falls
- ✓ Property Description regulations

3 Pricing policy and earning potential

It is generally accepted that short term and holiday rentals should generate a higher return than long term rentals. With this in mind, we will look at setting realistic expectations, which can be notoriously difficult for all new industries.

Long versus short term rentals

Firstly, it is essential to understand the difference in revenue predictability between long and short term rentals. Once the property is rented out to a long term tenant, the landlord has an almost guaranteed revenue stream for the duration of the agreement. There are provisions in place which govern pay, notice periods and vacation processes. The short term rentals function more like hotels and serviced apartments where there is no guarantee that all available days will be booked, paid for and occupied.

As you would expect, this key element affects the expected revenue, and may narrow the gap between long and short term rentals.

The above paragraph applies more to second properties available for rent throughout the year, and is less significant for primary residences which are only available when the owners travel for business or leisure. In these cases, the discrepancy factor is irrelevant as the property cannot be rented out to a long term tenant anyway.

Owner or agency managed

The second aspect to be taken into consideration is the cost of managing the entire process. If the owner is in charge of everything, then the cost is significantly lower than the cost of having a specialised agency doing all the legwork. However, specialised agencies may be the best option given their extensive experience and the full range of services that they can offer. This decision has multiple implications and I have dedicated a separate chapter to explain the pros and cons of going through an agency.

Pricing structure

When the price is right, everything goes well. The hosts receive fair compensation for their effort, while the guests receive the expected product. It is neither the place nor the scope of this guide to teach the in-depth mechanics of pricing a product although the elements below must be considered.

- Similar accommodation in the area - both short term rentals and traditional industries like hotels
- Location. Central areas are always in high demand.
- Size, features and equipment. Size does matter and character sells very well.
- Property condition
- Time of year. Christmas, Easter, summer or winter holidays can influence the price
- Important events in the local calendar. Think Paris Fashion Week, the Rio Carnival or the World Cup.

The above pricing elements offer different contributions to the mix but the top three are location, similar properties on offer and the size, features and equipment offered.

When used correctly, the above list will generate quite accurate rates but this must be a constant concern as the market is changing all the time. I have seen many hosts resisting to any changes in the price just to suffer a revenue loss because the market moved from their price.

Once all elements have been priced, step back and look at whether the result makes sense from a commercial point of view and it matches your business goals. Ultimately, the price itself has little relevance if not placed in the desired context. In other words, it doesn't matter much if the realistic price comes in at say $150 per day, but your expectation and price target is closer to say $300 per day.

In order to get a first impression about the potential revenue, you must search online for short term accommodation offers in your local area. Look for properties with a similar number of bedrooms, bathrooms, size and features. It doesn't have to be identical, but similar enough to be representative for the category you are after.

Once you have formed an initial opinion, it is a good idea to contact two or three short term letting agencies and ask them to assess the revenue potential for your property. The offer will certainly come in at a lower level and this is normal as the rental price must include also the agency's profit margin. This mark-up can vary greatly depending on the kind of agency (full management or service delivery only) and can be anywhere between 10% and 100%.

In other words, if the agency offers you $100 per day, you can expect to see a selling price of between $110 and $200 if they will start promoting your property. At first this can be confusing, but the rule of thumb is that full management is the most expensive agreement and the mark-up is usually above 25%. Again, this may change as the industry is extremely dynamic and margins fluctuate greatly. I explain more about this in the chapter about agencies.

However, at this stage all you need is a ballpark figure to see if you may be happy with the earning potential.

The initial research above should provide a pretty good picture about the realistic price level for your unit and you can now decide if the price is something you would consider.

I receive a lot of enquiries about specific pricing examples and my answer is always similar to the one given in the above paragraphs. This approach is designed to avoid a natural trap, the benchmarking allure which can lead to mispricing and a loss in the market just because at a certain point in time a certain city area was showing one price or another. By following the approach explained in the previous paragraphs, the owners can get a sense of where the price levels are and adjust their expectations accordingly.

There is also another reason to stay away from single price points. I often see how the price points for the same property are event or season driven. You can have the same two-bedroom flat in Kensington, London advertised at $150 per day in August then at $200 per day during the Christmas period and then again going to $120 per day for a quick sell if the owners are in a hurry to vacate for an unexpected business trip.

There is one more approach to take into consideration in order to complete the pricing process and form a good idea about the earning potential of your property. The spread between the long term and short term rental prices for similar properties in the market can be a good indicator. The numbers vary greatly and spreads can be as high as three times the long term rental price, but look for averages to smooth out the outliers.

For example, if you own a four-bedroom property in a certain area of the city, compare the rate spread for at least five or ten similar units in the same area. This ensures that levels at the extreme end are not skewing your results and that you have a good idea about the price you could realistically ask for your property. Once you find the "sweet spot", you can start adding price increments linked to unique features your property may have like views, a balcony, garden, high-end media systems or even a cinema, sauna or swimming pool.

It is worth mentioning that this should not be a one-off effort. As explained above, prices move constantly and the more in tune you are with the fluctuations, the better your revenue stream will look.

Chapter Checklist

✓ Check the average price for similar properties in your local area

✓ Find the average spread between the long term and short term rentals in your local area

✓ Be aware of the events taking place nearby and the time of the year when prices tend to fluctuate

✓ Obtain two or three offers from short term rental agencies and ask about the final market price

✓ Factor in all costs into the final price (property setup and cleaning, advertising, check in/out)

4 Health & safety and risk management

It is our nature to see only the bright side of a deal and to be oblivious to the inherent risks that every business carries. This is a general concern at all levels and I have seen quite a few business plans affected by unforeseen circumstances which could have been easily taken into account.

When working with and for people, the service delivery risks fall into two main categories: the legal requirements and good practice and guidance. While there is a clear distinction between them, the general aim is to protect all parties involved in the deal and to assist the property owner in the process of renting out the unit. A host must also make provisions and be prepared to deal with damage, noisy guests, loud parties and maintenance issues that can affect the guests' experience.

It never ceases to amaze me how many things can go wrong during a stay, and this is not always caused by any faults but because the guests are not familiar with the environment or because they have a completely different lifestyle and use of the equipment available. It is also sometimes the case that the property owner overlooks an important aspect assuming that it is neither obvious nor general practice.

It is always best to think that all reasons why people stay in hotels will also apply to you. Business or leisure, your guests will be in town for an unlimited number of reasons and they come from all walks of life. Some are careful and considerate, while others cannot care less about the state of the property.

Some will carefully read the host's instructions manual while others will ignore it completely and then mess with the equipment and then complain about it. Some will enjoy a quiet stay while others will throw a noisy party, damage the place and alienate your neighbours. Some will leave the place spotless and with a thank you note while others will stain your carpets, scratch your brand new kitchen worktop or rip the fabric on your sofa in the living room.

The more you work in the industry, the more examples you can add to an ever-growing list of damages, incidents and potential complaints and requests for compensation. Also, the business has intrinsic risks to be added on top of those resulting from normal use during the occupation.

Below, I have compiled a list of common incidents, complaints and compensation requests I had to deal with over the years, and although the collection is not exhaustive, you will undoubtedly understand the importance of this chapter:

- Financial compensation because upon arrival, the guests claim that the property is not as advertised or described during the marketing process.
- Refusal to pay for the damage cover guarantee on the grounds that there was no mention of it at the booking stage.
- Refusal to sign any rental agreement before viewing and inspecting the property.
- Full refund request because the guest couldn't find the key to the door to the backyard and the entire trip was based on access to that area of the house.

- Complaint and compensation because the internet connection doesn't support the streaming and usage capacity expected.
- Relocation and refund because the beds are either narrower or shorter than expected.
- Compensation for damages caused by a loose fitted carpet on the stairs.
- Compensation for discomfort caused by the smell of pets in the house.
- Discount for the first day because the meet & greet at check in was delayed.
- Discount request because the washing machine is not equipped with a dryer module.
- Requests for complimentary daily linen and towels change. Complaints if not offered.
- Discount because the number of keys provided is less than expected.
- Discount for the inconvenience caused by a faulty alarm panel.
- Financial compensation for scalds due to the shower water being too hot.
- Complaint because some storage space was taken by the host's belongings.
- Complaint for not providing enough crockery and cutlery for entertaining at home.
- Relocation because guests are inconvenienced by neighbours' resident cats.
- Relocation and refund because the block of flats doesn't have an elevator.
- Discount request because the carpets are stained in places or some walls have scuffs on them.
- Revenue loss through damages after large parties.
- Relocation and or refund for faulty boilers or other heating devices.

- Difficult relationships with neighbours caused by inconsiderate guests.
- Letters from the council if guests are inconveniencing your neighbours in any way.

I am sure that the above examples are significant and explain the need for very careful planning and for taking the risk management element very seriously.

For Health & Safety regulations, given the current fragmentation of the market, it is important to note that taking advice from the local authorities is always a good place to start. Also, go around and ask the short term rental agencies about their policies regarding accidents, damages and risk to the property and they should be able to advise you on this. During my years in the industry I have seen big differences between what is expected and what is delivered and this is generally caused by the cultural gaps which are inherent in this industry. However, ignorance won't make much of a difference when things go bad and the consequences can be very costly.

It is again important to be aware that this is not a legal guide and the advice herein is just a guidance to put you on the right track and to provide you with the tools to make your product as safe and as profitable as possible.

For regulated practices like hotels and serviced apartments, the subject is very well defined and managed by trained and qualified personnel. Given the existent similitudes between short term rentals and the hotel industry we can say that a good part of the rules apply to both businesses with quite a few particulars influencing the short term rentals market.

Regardless of what type of accommodation is on offer the list of actions below should be part of the property setup at all levels (local rules may take precedence but for this area no effort should be spared to have as complete a list as possible).

✓ All properties must have a valid Gas Safety Certificate (where applicable)
✓ Installation and maintenance of smoke detectors
✓ Consideration given to the provision of evacuation instructions in case of fire emergency
✓ Provision of a basic First Aid kit (check expiration date for each item) and provide its location
✓ Provision of a list with the local numbers for gas, fire, medical and police emergency support
✓ Ensure that all fixtures and fittings are in good working order and where applicable, are firmly attached to walls, floors, doors or the required support
✓ Provision of keys that are in good working order for all doors in the house where guests have access
✓ Attention paid to not locking out rooms as "off bounds" if containing essential equipment where guests may be required to go. Internet routers and alarm and heating control panels are the usual suspects
✓ Ensure that the house alarm (where available) is in good working order and emergency contacts are available in case of alerts or faults

- ✓ Check to ensure that all equipment is in good working order. This includes heating, hot water, kitchen and audio-TV-internet equipment, vacuum cleaners, hair dryers and any other electric appliances you offer
- ✓ If you accept families then walk around the house and identify hazards like sharp edges or corners, faulty sockets, exposed wires, loose fixtures and anything that can cause trouble to small children
- ✓ Be careful not to leave any heavy items on the top shelves out of reach of your guests
- ✓ Put up signs if any area of the house may become slippery when wet (kitchen, bathroom, and terrace)
- ✓ Put together an accurate list of the property's features and amenities. This list should be the same on all distribution channels
- ✓ Provision of a list with the contact names and numbers to call in case of technical faults and customer service support
- ✓ Inform your guests about the presence of any CCTV system in operation and specify the areas including terraces and gardens
- ✓ Make a list of all equipment with known minor faults or quirks. Temperamental locks, old light switches, warped sash windows or SANIFLO toilets are some of the most common
- ✓ Be very specific about your permission for smoking and wearing outside shoes inside and also what your policy is on parties of any kind in your property
- ✓ Provide a complete troubleshooting guide for dealing with equipment faults, jammed locks, broken windows and burst pipes
- ✓ Commit to maximum resolution times in case of maintenance faults and for any support requests from your guests

✓ Prepare an accurate description of your property and mention rooms and bed sizes in all your marketing channels. Do not remove too much of the normal clutter

We all know that regardless of the amount of preparation going into every stay, there will be occasions when things go wrong and you as the owner need to have a very specific action plan in place in order to deal with the situation in a quick, open and efficient manner. Much more will be explained in the chapters dedicated to Damages and Maintenance Support but for now it is suffice to say that the above areas must definitely be a part of your house setup.

Although it looks like a big task, the reality is that once the blueprint is ready, all subsequent rentals will use the same setup so it is important to do it right from the first time. Keep an eye on items with expiration dates like Gas Safety Certificates and First Aid box content. Also, ensure that contact telephone numbers and addresses are up to date and that all battery operated equipment like smoke detectors and remote controls are checked regularly.

Chapter Checklist

For this chapter, it is sufficient to follow the list above.

5 The rental agreement

A written and signed agreement is the only legally binding document between the host and the guests. Without it, the property owner has very limited protection and almost no support in case of a charge back (where the guests instruct their bank to cancel the payment and get the money back).

I have discussed this subject at length many times with different people and although the form and content vary greatly, there is unanimous agreement that every property owner must obtain a signed copy from each group of guests.

Therefore, in this chapter we will not discuss the merits of having an agreement but rather what you should aim to include in your personalised version. If you decide to give the property to an agency to manage, then they should provide you with a template agreement. Even if this is the case, it is good to read it carefully and confirm that it includes in one way or another all clauses mentioned below.

Even though the following paragraphs offer essential guidance on how to put together a good agreement, the explanation will address the topics at a concept level. Given the importance of such document I strongly advise you to seek legal advice so that the final format will have all the terms and conditions for watertight protection.

Before listing the main areas to be covered in this agreement, let's see what can go wrong before, during and after arrival so that the role of the agreement becomes clear.

Imagine that someone books your flat and you complete the pre-arrival process (we will look at this in detail later in a different chapter). The guest then refuses to sign any Rental Agreement until they arrive at the property and promises to do this immediately after viewing the house. What can happen (and it has happened to my teams quite a few times in reality) is that upon arrival and after viewing the flat, your guests refuse to check in because of a variety of reasons related to size, condition, clutter and all subjective perception reasons. In this case, without a signed agreement, you have a very small chance of keeping the money and it is almost certain that the guests will try to claim a refund. You have lost the revenue and the amount of time and money invested in the pre-arrival process. Add to this the opportunity cost of renting out to someone else and the total loss can become significant.

Let's say now that the guests didn't sign any agreement, arrived and checked in but in the process have damaged an item and also organised a big party which resulted in numerous complaints from your neighbours. Without the same signed agreement and a complete check-in process (explained in detail later in a different chapter) there isn't much you can do to recover the replacement or repair costs.

From my experience, I can say that every time something unexpected happens, it requires a significant amount of time and resources to put things right and to find the most equitable solution. In the absence of these key documents the task is almost impossible.

Look at the Rental Agreement as the only safety net available. The better it is, the more likely you are to have a trouble-free experience.

Now that we have explained the importance of such document let's see the key articles any agreement should have in order to offer the desired protection.

Always use the first page for the following key identifiers (there are quite a few more that may be used but these are a must-have on all agreements):

- Names of both the host and the lead guest
- The full address of your property
- The arrival and departure dates
- The total number of guests
- The names and ages of all guests
- The next destination

This set of data is very important as the entire document links into these fields and in case of disputes this is the start of all enquiries and investigations.

If you want, you can add more fields like a unique booking ID (useful for putting together a database), property setup (bedrooms, bathrooms, number and size of beds, available equipment) or even an empty box for additional comments.

Once the document has the above identifiers, you can start building the rules book governing the business relationship between you (the Host) and your guests.

Always make it clear in a short paragraph that the core of this agreement is for access to the unit in exchange of the money paid by the guest(s).

It is essential to add that this is not a standard tenancy agreement and does not offer any exclusive possession rights to your guest(s).

For all of the following articles it is important to use this format:

- State what you expect
- Clarify what happens if the requirement is not met

For example, explain that you need to identify the lead guest and only a photo ID will do. Then clarify that in the absence of a positive identification, the booking may be cancelled without refunding the amount paid.

Arrival, check-in and access to the property

Explain briefly what the process is and what documents will be needed upon arrival. It is essential to identify the lead guest so ask for a photo ID (in most cases a passport is the best option but local residents may only carry with them their driving licence or other form of ID.

Payment Terms

You need to explain clearly what costs are taken care of by you as a host. This subject can include the gas and electricity at the property, the specialised cleaning of the common areas and any other costs associated with living at the property. Here you must also clarify the circumstances and the processing of potential refunds, details about managing the damage cover guarantees you may want to hold for the duration of the stay and in general anything involving payments for your services.

The rest of the rental agreement will contain articles about the obligations both the host and the guest agree to observe and to take responsibility for. In no particular order, they fall into these categories (N.b the list is not exhaustive and articles may be included as the owner may see necessary):

For your guests

- The agreement does not grant any legal rights in relation to the property
- The lead guest accepts full responsibility for securing the house and for managing the access keys and alarm (where applicable) at all times
- Guest is not allowed to conduct business from the premises, to use it for illegal or immoral purposes or for consuming, selling or keeping illegal substances at the property
- No animals are allowed inside without the express written approval of the owner
- If you do not allow parties or large gatherings then a clause about this must be included

- The owners and their representatives must be allowed access to the house if needed (upon receiving 24 hours' notice)
- The property must be kept clean and all cooking, cleaning and rubbish disposal must be done according to the owner's instructions
- There must be clarity about what happens at the end of the stay. The guests must vacate the property on the day when the agreement ends
- Establish that the costs for the damages attributable to the guest will be recovered from the damage cover guarantee held for the duration of the stay

For you as a host

- The host provides access and use of the property as per the booking details
- All fixtures and fittings are in good working order and do not pose any danger to the occupier
- The property has all necessary equipment so that the guests do not have to source services for domestic activities such as cooking, cleaning and washing
- The property will be clean (hotel standard) and all guidance manuals made available upon arrival
- The host must provide a schedule with the agreed resolution times for support in case of maintenance emergencies

Other clauses

- Any potential extra charges and the reasons for them

- A termination clause in case of breach of contract (specific notice period is needed here)
- The status of lost property (how long it will be kept and what will happen if not collected)
- Rules for communicating with guests. Clarify how this will happen and if you need the lead guest to respond or acknowledge in any way to your communication. There will be instances when you need the guests to respond (meeting for keys at the end of the stay) and there will be instances when you may have to take action with or without their express consent (if you need to visit the property to pick up the post or other important documents and the guests have not responded to your notice).
- Circumstances out of your control when any inconvenience caused to the guests will not be your responsibility. You can think of burglary, flooding due to extreme weather conditions, earthquakes, social unrest or similar events and add them to the list.

Finally, your agreement must have space for names, signatures and date for you and your guests. You should give one copy to your guests and retain the other for your records.

IMPORTANT NOTE

Depending on the country of your residence, you may have to report to the authorities the names, ages, reason for travel and the intended next destination for all your guests. In any case, it is good practice to keep these records for at least one year or for the duration required by law.

I am sure that by now it is well understood how complex and important this document is and while a basic version can be put together with relative ease, the truth is that you need professional advice to create a professionally written document.

Chapter checklist

✓ Create a rental agreement template by following the clauses suggested in this chapter

✓ Alternatively, either seek professional advice or use the template suggested by a rental agency (if you intend to use their services to fully manage your house)

✓ Think and write down as many examples as possible of where things can go wrong and ensure that you include clauses for all of them in your rental agreement

6 Owner or agency managed

This subject comes up very often in my conversations and truth be told, there are pros and cons for each option.

At first glance it is obvious that the profit margin may be far higher when going alone, but for this business model the agencies can add real value to the table and their fees are well justified.

To start with, you have to decide if you have the time and inclination to get involved in the marketing and operation of the business. To answer this question you have to see yourself doing the following:

- Creating, submitting and regularly updating the online property profile on all marketing distribution channels
- Dealing with enquiries
- Doing the due diligence to discern the quality of your potential guests and asses potential risks
- Taking bookings, managing payments, damage cover guarantees and sending out booking confirmations, rental agreements and invoices
- Arranging arrivals and meet and greet for your guests
- Preparing the property for the stay (inventory, photos, cleaning, bed setup)
- Organising support during the stay
- Dealing with maintenance issues
- Taking and managing complaints

- Investigating compensation and refund requests
- Dealing with out of hours emergencies
- Arranging the meet for keys upon departure
- Returning the property to its initial state after departure (inventory, photos, cleaning)
- Dealing with damages, repairs and late charges
- Returning the damage cover guarantees
- Managing your reputation on social media channels

From the list above you can understand that this task may not be lucrative if all you want is to rent your property out for a few weeks every year. Given the lead time from listing to booking, the busy correspondence before arrival, the number of challenges and time intensive service support needed during the stay and finally, the risk of having to deal with damages, charges, complaints and the host of inherent activities, it is easy to understand that specialised agencies may offer a better solution.

If, however, the above list is just your cup of tea then you will benefit from the following:
- Full control over the quality of your product and service delivery
- Increased flexibility in terms of adjusting the price to adapt to market fluctuations
- Much shorter response and resolution times in case of complaints and compensation requests
- Direct contact with the guests who will rent out your place

- Meeting people from all over the world

- Upgrading your existing skillset in so many directions

- Monitoring the condition of your property more closely

- Increasing your profit margin significantly

- Better control of your social media profile and reputation

Before deciding in favour of going solo or asking an agency to represent you, there are two other aspects to consider, the agencies' profit margins and the different packages they offer.

Virtually all agencies operate based on three models and some of them offer all of them depending on your needs:

- Advertise Only

- Limited Service

- Fully Managed

For 'Advertise Only', you will only pay a listing and marketing fee. The agency will promote your property and charge you a marketing fee which is usually between 5% - 10% of the total price. Prices may vary, but this is the range you can reasonably expect. Once the sale is complete you will take over and, except for the first four points in the list I have introduced on the previous pages, you will have to deal with the rest of the booking process.

If you choose the 'Limited Service' then on top of the above 'Advertise Only', the agency may offer a meet and greet and payment support. However, you are still left with many responsibilities in the areas of property setup, maintenance and customer service support and finally the process of decommissioning the property once the stay is over. The other variation of the Limited Service is the 'Operations Only' package where the company takes over from you once you have rented out your place.

They will prepare the property, meet and greet your guests and offer maintenance and customer service support for the entire duration of the stay. All you have to do is promote and rent your property out. For these models, the agency fees tend to be in the range of 10%-15% of the total rental amount but the workload for you as the host will be greatly reduced.

The most comprehensive service package is the full management of your property and this includes everything from the first list. The agency will sign a services contract with you; will meet you for a detailed discussion about your requirements and then a professional property instructions manual will be created. Once this is done you can sit back, relax and let the agency promote, sell, prepare, maintain and manage your property for you.

If you decide to go with a Fully Managed package then researching the following areas for your chosen agent will help you find the right company to work with:

✓ *What is their internal structure and who is in charge of your property?*
   You should be looking for organisations with well-defined departments and roles like reservations, account management,

property management (maintenance), a housekeeping department and customer service front desk. Ideally, you want just one point of contact for your day to day needs and an emergency contact number for out of hours support.

✓ *What marketing and distribution channels are used?*
Don't forget that nothing starts unless you find someone to pay you the money and rent the property from you. A serious agency should be able to show membership in one or two major distribution channels (examples and names will be listed in a later chapter), a very successful company website and a great social media presence.

✓ *What is their social media reputation?*
Browse the forums and websites such as Trip Advisor, Facebook or Twitter to gauge the overall reputation of the agent. Look for comments on response times, support quality, ability to screen guests prior to arrival, average quality of the properties in their portfolio (this will give you a good picture of the segment of travellers booking their inventory), management response to complaints and whether the responders would use them again.

✓ *What processes are in place to deal with maintenance issues, complaints and emergencies?*
It is essential to assess the agent's ability to step in and deliver a good service when things go wrong. Successful companies have dedicated maintenance departments, a solid list with third party contractors, well

trained front desk agents and consistent training programmes on customer service. Make sure you have a clear picture of your responsibilities and what charges you will have to absorb in case of equipment faults or out of hours incidents.

✓ *What processes are in place for ensuring the security of your property?*
You should ask questions related to the way the access keys are managed, how they screen and veto their own employees with access to the property, what processes are in place to ensure that the unit is locked and protected at all times and what is the briefing given to the guests upon arrival.

✓ *What is the pricing process and how long is the payment cycle?*
Clarify the pricing process and ask the agent to justify their offer. Always obtain prices from two or three other agents and compare their pricing strategies. Enquire about the way the agent will pay you and make sure you understand and accept the amounts, percentages and timelines. Everything can be negotiated and the more you understand the market the better you are positioned to obtain a fair deal. It is very important to have clarified what happens when the equipment in your house develops a fault so that you know what to expect in terms of cost.

✓ *What are the Terms and Conditions that guests have to sign?*
This is the Rental Agreement we have seen in the previous chapters. As mentioned already, this is the only binding document between you

and the guest and the content of the articles will offer protection and peace of mind to both parties. Refer to the checklist and the points detailed in the Rental Agreement chapter for advice on what to look for in the agent's copy.

Never forget that THE CONTRACT IS BETWEEN YOU AND THE GUEST and that the agency is just a facilitator. This means that the rights and responsibilities captured in the document refer directly to you and your guests and the agency's duty of care cannot replace the obligations you and the guests have for the duration of the agreement.

✓ *What is the pricing policy?*

Hotels and established serviced apartments businesses have a very strong revenue management process in place to adjust rates for seasonality, special events in town, natural no-show rates and other circumstances with the ability to influence prices. It is, however, very early days for the short term letting industry and this may not be readily available but look to find at least a proactive approach to extracting as much revenue as possible from every potential booking.

Now having a broad view of the options at your disposal it is down to you to assess your own circumstances and decide which road to take.

The number of professional short term rental agencies is growing rapidly all over the world. There are already very big agencies such as Airbnb® which are known all over the world and at the same time, there are many smaller businesses with boutique-style operations but with a much more personalised service.

Before concluding this chapter, I want to say a few words about the practice of using more than one agency. Quite a few of our current hosts are in business with several agencies and this is done for maximising the exposure and distribution potential. There isn't anything wrong with this practice and as long as the selection process is consistent for all agencies you can expect to benefit from a wider audience. However, if that's the case, then a very accurate calendar management (discussed in detail in the next chapter) must be put in place and this falls into your set of responsibilities. Without up to date visibility of all available dates there is the risk of bookings overlap which can affect the top line and implicitly, the bottoms line of your business and also cost a lot in terms of loss of reputation.

Chapter checklist
- ✓ Take stock of your skillset in relation to the tasks needed to manage this business model
- ✓ Decide which model works best for you from the three models presented
- ✓ If you will use an agency start researching at least three offers and compare their competence with the use of the questions explained in this chapter
- ✓ Decide if you want to use more than one agency in the process and make the necessary arrangements

7 Calendar management and Availability

When you set your expectations on the odds of renting your property out exactly on the days when you are away, you must take into consideration the following elements:

- Booking system - automated or enquiry based?
- The minimum LOS (length of stay) for a booking
- The average booking lead time depending on size, season and various events in town
- Back-to-back bookings -. careful timing needed for transitioning from the leaving party to those arriving on the same day
- How much notice is needed to accept new bookings
- How much notice you will accept when guests want to cancel a confirmed booking

All of these elements will impact your revenue if not managed carefully and we will see how to approach each one of them so that you maximise your occupancy rate.

Booking system - automated or enquiry based?

While the automation of online travel agencies like booking.com or expedia.com will increase the chance of getting bookings fast, it is worth mentioning that there won't be any screening or assessing how suitable a guest is for your property. If you set your booking acceptance on enquiries only then all potential guests will have to call or email to ask for details like availability, check-in arrangements or payment methods. As a rule of thumb, if you want a quick booking then automating the process is best but the relationship with the travel agency is usually done through an agent and it is not readily available for individual operators.

The minimum LOS (length of stay) for a booking

This control is very important for filtering enquiries and should be considered carefully. If you accept one-day stays and you have a one bedroom flat then your main competitors are the local hotels and serviced apartments. Also, one or two night stays increase the likelihood of people booking your apartment for weekend parties which in itself is a risk as you will have to decide whether you want to accept that or not. When looking to set this up it is always a good idea to ask around for the average length of stay your local agents have. This will be your guide and also needs to factor in the size of your property. Very short stays are usually for business and emergency travel while longer durations (5 days and more) will bring in the leisure and relocation segments. Exceptions can and will always happen but the strategy must consider the trends and averages. There is another aspect to discuss and this refers to events.

When Fashion Week is in town, you can expect an increase in the number of 5-8 days enquiries for instance. The World Cup booking pace will follow the game fixtures and you can expect a constant stream of enquiries with peaks around the opening and closing days as well as on match days. Also, the closer you get to the final, the more people will be in town.

As you can see, the LOS game is more of an art than a science and only experience will tell you what the optimal setup for your property is. Keep in mind though that the higher the LOS, the smaller the pool of enquiries becomes and the slope becomes apparent when going higher than 10 days.

Average booking lead time depending on season and various events in town

It is well known that booking patterns vary and this is usually dictated by the purpose of travel. Business people have ever-changing diaries and very often this will lead to last minute booking requests. On the other side of the spectrum you have the leisure segment with travellers starting shopping around months in advance to find the best rates.

High impact events like the Olympic Games, the World Cup or even the Fashion Week have longer than usual booking lead times.

You should take these patterns into consideration when deciding how early you will open up your calendar for new bookings.

For instance, say that your property will be vacant from the 1st of July for two weeks and you think of opening up your calendar for new bookings on the 20th of June – this means that you have only nine days left for the travel portals to find your property, send enquiries, arrange payments, screen your guests, organise the property setup and meet and greet. If you have also a minimum notice of say three days, this leaves just six days to complete the same process.

According to the booking patterns we have described, the most probable enquiries will come from business people (if you have a small, e.g. one or two-bedroom flat) or from last minute, emergency travellers. You will most probably lose the leisure segment with bookings far in advance.

In general, the further ahead you know the available days for your property, the better your chances are for securing better deals. If instead of the 20th of June, you open the calendar on the 1st of May you have two months to market, sell and set up your property. Obviously, the more availability you add to the calendar the more flexible you can be and the importance of lead times tends to decrease. When you are only at the beginning of your journey, it is always best to start advertising your property as early as possible. You will have time to adjust this as you progress and understand the market better.

Back-to-back bookings

This can cause headaches if not managed properly. You have to put in place very clear standards for arrival and departure times so that enough time is allocated for the transition between the two bookings. If you manage your own property then a departure time of 10am and 3pm arrival time are generally accepted in the industry. You will have, without a doubt, early arrival requests but the temptation to accept anything just to make the sale must not affect the quality of the pre-arrival process. Always ensure that the departure is properly taken care of before committing to an early arrival.

How much notice is needed for new bookings and cancellations?

We have touched on this in a previous paragraph and the primary focus here should be on clarity and transparency. You need to let your guests know how early before arrival they can cancel if their travel plans have changed. Equally, the controls you set in your property profile will dictate how many days in advance of the desired arrival date your guests can book. The higher the numbers in both categories the more limited the market is, but ultimately it is a matter of individual preference and each property owner will have a different tolerance to these numbers.

Chapter checklist

- ✓ Decide what dates you want to make available in your calendar
- ✓ Contact a few agencies and enquire about the average length of stay for a similar size and type of property. Set the minimum LOS for your property
- ✓ Research the important events in your city in relation to the dates available in your calendar
- ✓ Open your calendar for new bookings as early as possible.

8 Marketing your property and managing expectations

The remaining chapters of this professional guide will deal with the actual product and will show you how to take an idea and change it into money. When managed properly, this should be a safe and profitable process for all parties involved.

I want to start by setting an important standard which you must adhere to in absolutely everything you will do from now on. Regardless of what process we will be looking at, it must be understood and accepted that the primary focus will be on the *management of guests' expectations*. All successful companies live and die by this "sword" which has so many edges. I can't emphasise enough how important it is to be aware of the power of expectations and how they affect us at every moment.

Before we address the main topic of this chapter let's take a brief walk down expectations lane and explore its meanders.

As we go along with our daily lives we continuously form opinions and experience emotions based on the way we imagine things and not on how they really are. For example, think of how we build our enthusiasm up for that cruise we always wanted to book and how once on board we feel disillusioned because we feel sea sick or claustrophobic or even bothered by the vibration of those immensely powerful engines. Equally, we all remember birthday presents and how some of them were less interesting than the others we were convinced we'll receive. Another classic example is the excitement build-up before a dinner at the best restaurant in town just to return disappointed by the meal size, waiting time or prices.

There is virtually no aspect of our lives that is immune to this phenomenon and the common denominator is the imagination which distorts our common sense and logic. The above examples can become equally exciting if the outcome is above our expectations. We go on a cruise fearing high waves and small cabins just to discover that we actually enjoy the constant move of the ship and the chic bedrooms. In the same vein, a much more treasured present for our birthdays can change our mood almost instantly while a better tasting meal than expected by attentive waiters can make our day.

What is interesting is that the expectations game works both ways and it can cause disappointment if the expectations were set too high or excitement if they are set too low. However, in the business world it is highly advisable to focus on delivering a consistent and predictable product and if the unexpected shows up, it is better to be on the upside.

In reality though there is a constant tug of war between the sales and the delivery of anything we produce around the world. The sales pitch must attract buyers by putting the product in the best possible light while the delivery will necessarily have the limitations of the actual product. All successful businesses have accepted that a fine balance between the two is the only sustainable strategy and this is evident in everything they do during the marketing stage.

What I want you to take from this introduction is that you have the duty of care to market your product in a way that is as close to reality as possible. In the long run this will help you to build a solid reputation and this in turn will contribute to a steady stream of income for years to come.

Now, let's go back to the job of understanding the best way to market our product which is the short term rental of our property. We will consider briefly the classic five Ps of marketing: product, place, promotion, price and profit.

It is understood that all marketing efforts will be conducted online and therefore the above mix must adapt to the realities of the internet community. If you want to adopt the terminology then remember that your PRODUCT must be sold in the right PLACE through an honest and accurate PROMOTION process and sold at the right PRICE to ensure the highest PROFIT.

You have total control over these levers and everything starts with the product itself. You will decide how your house will look for the guests, what areas will be off bounds, how much clutter you will leave behind and what storage space and kitchen equipment your guests will have access to. Once the house is ready it is again entirely up to you how the service delivery will look in relation to the pre-arrival, during the stay and the post-departure touch points with your guests.

The guest cycle is entirely under your control and this is really good news. There isn't anything here outside your control and the entire marketing mix can and should create good value for money for guests and an excellent reputation for you, the property owner.

We will use this approach for managing expectations and creating the best marketing mix in everything we will discuss from now on. Every step of the way must reflect your effort to supply your potential guests with enough data to make an informed decision and then enjoy a service level in line with expectations which are carefully controlled by you all the way.

The property profile (photos, description, size, setup, clutter)

In the online industry it is recognised that photos are the most important weapon in your arsenal and they should be used wisely. The reason for this is that they will provide a large contribution to the decision-making process. Given their importance, many people are attracted to the idea of enhancing the originals to show the property in a far better light and even editing them so that they improve the selling opportunities. While this may be true and some guests will indeed book because of your amazing photos, the reality is that setting expectations that are not realistic will lead to disappointment, complaints, negative feedback and a damaged reputation in social media. In some countries there are laws protecting against misrepresenting a product and you may be even fined if it is proved that the discrepancy has affected the sale.

For example, if your house is normally cluttered and full of family photos, decorative objects, pieces of furniture and other personal items, do not remove them completely during the photoshoot. If your house will look like a hotel room or serviced apartment on the website then imagine your guests' reaction upon arrival when they discover the reality. In the holiday rentals business people really like to live like locals and therefore accept a house with character. While I am not an advocate of lots of clutter and very busy rooms I have certainly seen how attractive it is for guests to live in the centre of someone else's home universe and to have access to their history, family photos, books and an entire collection of objects defining a certain lifestyle.

Also, if you choose to add a description of the property with your photos, you should be careful with the use of words like "fabulous", "amazing", "majestic", "unique" or "incredible" unless this is indeed a true representation of certain features of your house. Going back to our building blocks, it is very easy and attractive to use superlatives to attract buyers but if your property is a 50 square meter, two-bedroom flat on the second floor of a 10-story block of flats next to a railway, describing it as a "fabulous development overlooking the shopping district" will be of minimal long-term value to you.

A good description complements your photos by adding accurate information about the real size of the rooms and beds (in square meters and centimetres), identifying your most attractive features (location, view, A/C, fireplace, swimming pool, sauna, art objects, etc...) and by listing all local attractions and points of interest your guests may be interested in.

A separate paragraph should contain the necessary information related to the guest cycle where the arrival, the stay and finally the departure processes must be explained. Include details such as check-in time, meet and greet and showing round, security checks during arrival (guests to show the payment card used for payment at the booking stage, signature check, individual ID, etc…), damage cover guarantees and cancellation policies (discussed in a later chapter).

Chapter checklist

- ✓ Photos showing how the property will look like *when guests arrive* and not after a major redecoration. Do not remove items from the room just to make it look more spacious if you know that you will return that item to the room and leave it there for your guests
- ✓ Be careful with the degree of processing that goes into the production of the final photos. If you work with an agency, be very clear about what you expect them to do and resist the temptation to make your flat look like a penthouse on 5th Avenue in New York. This will only create unrealistic expectations and while the sale will take place, upon arrival your guests may be very disappointed and either ask for compensation, full refund or even worse, they won't say anything but leave a very damaging review on all-important social media channels.
- ✓ In your description, give as much useful information as possible. People come from all over the world and standards are very different.
- ✓ The same care must be reflected in all your telephone and email sales conversations. Accuracy is the name of the game and although you

will undoubtedly put your property in the best light possible - the closer to reality you stay the better long-term prospects become.

✓ In general the best levers available are location, proximity to places of interest and how well the property layout fits into the guests' requirements (bedrooms, bed setup and features). Keep close to these and you will do well

9 Multiple occupation and the average rate per guest

This topic is little discussed and even less understood, although it impacts the type of guests you will have, the burden on your property, the volume of interactions with your neighbours and ultimately the overall guest experience.

The idea is that in theory, you can maximise your chances to rent your property out if you accept more guests than your house is normally designed for and furnished to accept. For example, think of bookings where 12 guests are sharing 3 bedrooms (normally occupied by say, 6 residents) and they have to use extra beds and sleep in the living room too.

In order to grasp this concept you have to think of the usual number of residents in the property and compare it with the total number of people you are happy to accept in a booking. For example, if you own a two bedroom house and you live there with your spouse and one child, your usual number is three. This will generate a certain amount of wear and tear on furniture and house objects, create a certain level of noise and rubbish and involve your family in a certain amount of interaction with your neighbours. You have designed and adapted your house for the lifestyle of three people sharing the entire house.

The larger your property is, the more study, dining or living rooms there are and therefore the higher the number of people who can potentially occupy it for short term rentals is.

This creates an interesting conundrum and in practice, the implications are not obvious. On the one hand the more guests you accept, the better chance you have of renting out the house but on the other hand this will increase the burden and wear and tear on your house, and by reducing the rate per guest you will open up your property to a different market segment. Let's say that you market your four bedroom house for $600 per day and that you have designed it to sleep five members of your family. If you will rent it out to a party of five guests, this brings the rate per guest to $120 per day.

However, if you adapt your house to accommodate two guests in each bedroom and also install an extra bed in the living room, you will accept parties of up to 10 guests and this brings the rate per guest down to $60 per day. Aside from the extra wear and tear, noise and increased interaction with your neighbours, your guests now pay a rate comparable maybe to hostels or 1-star and 2-star equivalent accommodation.

You will therefore receive the same amount each day but the mix of people staying with you will be of a different quality - the low-budget travel kind.

We can argue that this is ultimately a matter of personal strategy but it is worth exploring the options and finding the right balance. This is because you will certainly return to your house after the trip and you won't want to find alienated neighbours, local council complaint letters and a tired house.

Chapter checklist

- ✓ Work out the rate per guest for your current property configuration
- ✓ Calculate the maximum capacity for your house (with extra beds and sofa beds)
- ✓ Find your comfort zone between the two levels. Take into account all aspects listed earlier in the chapter like neighbours, noise, wear and tear and the market segment you are targeting.

10 Payment methods, terms and the damage cover guarantee

Today, all transactions are conducted online and if you decide to manage the property on your own it is important to know how to set up your payment cycle for processing payments and refunds.

If you want to keep things simple, you can accept bank transfers from guests' accounts to your own account. This is generally the best option if you don't want to be exposed to potential payment card fraud and charge backs. The drawback is that you may lose quite a few deals as people look for convenience and speed which are both provided by payment card systems like VISA®, MasterCard®, American Express®, Diners Club® or JCB® as the major card services. If you choose to accept debit and credit cards, you have to sign up for membership services with payment processing companies and there will be fees you will have to pay for every transaction. You will also have to setup an online payment gateway or you may be able to accept payments over the phone, which makes the service more personalised.

Regarding the actual payment terms, you can charge a certain percentage from the total amount at the time of booking and then take the balance closer to the arrival date. This may be a good incentive for guests who book well in advance because they may be reluctant to pay the entire amount months before arrival.

When the booking is made less than 14 days before the arrival date I recommend taking the full amount to reduce the likelihood of cancellations or amendment requests.

Given the character of the short term rental business model, cancellations are very challenging for you as a host because you may not be able to find an alternative solution and you risk losing the revenue. This is especially true if you rent your house for a limited period, usually for less than two or three weeks every year. Almost all agencies have very strict rules for refunds and in general, once made, bookings cannot be cancelled without incurring a cancellation fee.

The closer you are to the arrival date the higher the cancellation fee is and in many cases guests are charged the full amount. If you work alone, this is entirely at your discretion but you must remember the lost opportunity cost if you refund the money and fail to find other guests. Sometimes you may be able to relist your property, and if you find someone else you can refund the initial guests, but again, this is something to be decided by you or in the event that you work with an agency, it is part of your agreement with them.

The concept of holding a damage cover guarantee is general practice everywhere and is designed to offer a certain degree of cover in case of damage or theft. It also creates an increased sense of responsibility for guests who will be more careful with your property. The amount you will be asking for depends on the amount of excess you have in your insurance contract and on the replacement cost of the content of your house which is made accessible to guests. As you have guessed already, house items tend to be expensive and when you have to deal with several damages, the total can escalate very quickly.

This means that if you want to be covered in any circumstances you have to use the insurance and damage cover guarantee together. In general, the damage cover guarantee size is the same as the amount you carry as excess in your insurance policy, which is the level of risk you agree to cover from your funds before the insurance kicks in so that the premium is lower. In the hotel and serviced apartments industry, the potential damage is relatively limited and because of this, the amount used for a deposit is small, in the range of $0 - $150. In the short term rentals industry, the amount can go higher and the amount you will be using is a personal decision. In theory, the higher it is the less insurance premium you pay and the guests will be more careful during their stay. The drawback is that the more money you hold, the less comfortable your guests become and this can be a barrier to the sales process. Damage cover guarantees are usually released after the departure inventory and it is important that you let your guests know at the booking stage how long this will take.

If you work with agencies then you have greater peace of mind as they are very good at managing payments and damage cover guarantees and all good ones have people trained to deal with damages and repairs.

I want to add a few considerations about accepting cash payments for the damage cover guarantee. This business requires much more trust than traditional hotels do because the industry is less regulated, and the interactions occur in isolated locations around town. Some guests are more comfortable paying in cash upon arrival once they meet someone and there is confirmation that the place is indeed available and ready for them. While this in itself is not necessarily a bad thing, you have to consider the logistics and the fact that you will have to agree how to return the money at the end of the stay. If you will not be in town this can be a problem and you may have to use the services of an electronic courier, although there will be a charge for the service.

Chapter checklist

- ✓ Decide which payments you want to accept
- ✓ If you accept cash, make it clear what currencies you accept and the deposit return timeframe
- ✓ Prepare the receipt template for accepting cash payments
- ✓ Put together a disclaimer about how you will deal with cancellations and refund requests
- ✓ Arrange the payment gateways with your bank (bank transfers and card acceptance)

11 Pre-arrival property setup

Congratulations! You have rented out your property and now you must deliver the product. Your guests are in the middle of arranging their travel and soon they will be knocking at your door.

Now you need to "deliver the goods" and central to this is how you prepare your house for this. If the property will be managed by an agency then check with them what the process is. While the steps may vary, it is important that all of the following areas are covered:

Property inventory

An inventory captures the condition of all fixtures and fittings in a property and supports the findings with detailed photos of all damaged items (marks, scratches, chips, stains and scuffs). Once signed by both parties, this is the accepted reference for all damage claims.

Professional versions are very time consuming and the cost tends to be high. It indeed captures everything but it is only meant to be used for the long-term letting business.

Short term rentals use a simplified version which has less detail but more photos and just captures the existing damage. If a fixture or fitting is not damaged then it won't be captured in the report. This simplifies the process and reduces the cost of preparing inventories every time there is a new booking. An inventory for a three bedroom property with two bathrooms, one living room and backyard shouldn't take longer than 1.5 hours to prepare.

Follow these simple steps for putting together a solid inventory:

- Walk around the house from left to right on every floor and write down all damages you find
- Capture each damaged area or item in two photos from different angles.
- Take a generic photo of each room in the house (studies, storage rooms included) to provide the big picture of the pre-arrival setup
- Take a photo with the property keys

When describing damage use words like *mark, scratch, chip, stain, crack, scuff* or *rip* to describe the type of damage. The supporting photos must be placed into context so that you can identify the room, the location and the size of the damage.

Once prepared you must hand over a copy to your guests and give them 24 hours to look around and come back to you if they find damage that is not captured in your document. The understanding must be that if no notice is received within the first 24 hours, the inventory is considered accepted by both parties and will become the reference for all disputes related to damages during the stay.

It is good practice to keep all inventories from past bookings so that you have continuity and reference in case of backdated claims.

Rental agreement

Once the booking is confirmed and paid for, you must send out a copy of the rental agreement to your guests as we have discussed in an earlier chapter. Guests have the obligation to print out, sign, scan and email it back to you before the arrival date. Remember that this is the only binding document between you and your guests.

Access keys, fobs and alarms

You should cut one set of access keys for each two guests you accept but not more than four sets. Always keep a fifth set with you and also give one set to a friend or neighbour, just in case. It is critical that you keep close tabs on keys, fobs and all related items. Make an inventory of all access areas and check to ensure that all locks work well. If you have a temperamental lock that you have always used, do not assume that your guests will be equally successful. There is nothing more costly and inconvenient than a call in the middle of the night from locked-out guests. Emergency locksmiths are notoriously expensive.

Alarm codes and fobs must be checked and clear setup instructions given to the guests. Even if the alarm is deactivated and must not be used, do not assume that guests will comply. People are curious and children are children, going around pushing buttons and pulling strings.

Instructions for your guests

You must prepare an instruction manual for your guests. Other than the photos and description, they don't know much else about your property and the manual must provide the following essential information:

- A one-mile radius map of your location (for transport links, restaurants and food shops).

- Emergency procedures and numbers to call

- Access to the property (alarms, locks, keys)

- Security rules to observe when leaving the house and overnight

- List of all off-bound areas in the house where guests don't have access

- Instructions for controlling the heating and hot water at the property

- Instructions for operating the TV, internet and the kitchen equipment

- List of house rules (for example no pets, no shoes inside, no smoking or no ceremonial fumigations)

- Rubbish disposal rules (some local councils have strict rules and will enforce this very strongly)

- Local info about transport links, places to visit and your preferred restaurants and shops

- Anything else that you believe will create a hassle-free experience for your guests

Beds setup and sleeping arrangements

Regardless of the party size, it is always good practice to make up all beds in the house. The bed set must consist of one mattress protector, one bed sheet, one duvet cover and pillows according to the size of the bed (one pillow for bunk and single beds, two pillows for all other sizes). Sofa beds and extra beds are usually made as beds only if requested or if a part of the rental package. If made up for arrival, then a similar bed set must be used.

When shopping for extra beds, the inflatable or foldable ones are your options. If your guests won't have to inflate and deflate the bed every day for access then they may be as reliable as the foldable ones. However, if the place you install them requires constant manipulation and storage then the foldable ones are far better as they last longer.

It is preferable to make up the beds hotel style with folded corners for bedsheets and the duvets tucked underneath the mattress. The goal is to have the bed dressed up neatly and without creases or any other folds. Check the internet for how-to videos on the subject.

The minimum quality standard for linen should be 150 thread count cotton, and the higher you go the better the feel is for guests. Once you go above 200 thread count, the difference is easily noticed. The same goes for duvet covers and pillow cases. The colour theme is entirely up to you and the vast majority of hospitality places have adopted a white colour scheme.

Towels, hairdryers and welcome packs

We have all experienced that warm and fluffy feeling when using hotel towels. The best results are achieved from 600 gsm cotton towels and you should aim to offer three sizes for each guest - hand towels, bath towels and bath sheets. Colour is again a personal choice and yes, white is again the favourite of hotels and serviced apartments.

The standard bathroom welcome packs contain soap, shampoo, moisturiser and toilet paper. For a richer experience, you can add protective shower caps, combs, sewing kits and gloves. Almost all properties provide hairdryers and you should have one available.

The kitchen welcome packs should contain washing up liquid, scourers, dishwasher tablets, detergent and the standard first day pack of tea, coffee, hot chocolate and sugar sachets.

Kitchen equipment, crockery, cutlery, glassware, pots and pans

As a rule of thumb, you have to provide enough crockery, cutlery and glassware for the maximum number of guests you will have staying at your house. Also, always provide 4-5 more as they may have their own people visiting. The minimum you have to provide is a wok, a standard frying pan and two or three pots. If you have expensive sets, I strongly recommend storing them away and purchasing standard sets from the local store. I have seen very expensive crockery sets ruined because one guest had chipped a plate and that pattern wasn't in production anymore. If you are uncomfortable with the idea of losing them then err on the safe side and put them safely away.

There is absolutely nothing wrong with offering a different set to your guests and many sets out there look great and do the job perfectly well for a very moderate price. There is only one exception, and this is when you are actually advertising your exquisite crockery and cutlery as a feature of your product. If that is the case, you obviously cannot replace them but make sure that you are insured and protected in case of damage.

In all modern kitchens, people expect to find a fridge and freezer, an oven and hob, a microwave oven, a kettle, a toaster, dishwasher and washing machine. However, this can vary greatly from country to country and the above setup is by no means how the kitchen should look like. It is always nice to have all mod cons but as long as you explain what is on offer during the booking stage then everything should be alright.

TV, internet and other audio-video equipment
It is entirely up to you what TV package you want to offer to your guests but you should aim to have as a minimum: a news channel, a movies channel, a kids channel and a shopping channel. I am sure that usually, the TV package is much more generous and this area should not cause any major concern. As a gentle reminder, do not forget to check the batteries on the remote control. You will be surprised to learn how many times I had to send my maintenance support out to change them. If you will manage the property on your own then you will cover the cost of going there or sending your tech support to attend.

The internet is a permanent feature in all big cities and is no longer seen as a luxury. However, you must not commit to certain speeds or usage capacity and the guests should be made aware of the concept of fair usage policy. In general, you should provide an internet connection good enough for browsing, checking emails and for accessing social media channels. A Wi-Fi connection is essential as most often your guests will have more than one device to connect to the internet.

If you will offer other audio-video equipment, make sure you explain how each system operates and that all remote controls will be available. From my experience I suggest avoiding a complicated setup or multiple remote controls as this is a sure way of running into problems and to cause annoyance to your guests. When this happens guess who will have to attend and fix the faults or user errors?

Storage space for guests

If the property is your primary residence you will have to leave behind almost all of your belongings and this is actually one of the selling points of the short term rental industry - to live like a local and experience their lifestyle. This means that most of your storage space is already taken by your belongings but consider that your guests will have luggage and therefore will need storage space.

The general rule is to free up storage space in each bedroom and the size is really linked to the number of people you will be renting your house to. Think of freeing up entire drawers as well as wardrobes. If this is not possible, you have to inform your guests in advance and as a minimum provide hanging rails for suits, dresses and coats.

Protecting your valuables and setting off-limits areas

We all have valuable items, heirlooms and objects carrying great emotional value to us and it is important to protect them from accidental damage or theft. I always advise owners to store away everything they wouldn't be comfortable losing. While we don't want to lose anything, it is one thing to have to replace a standard porcelain plate and another thing to find a unique wedding gift vase chipped or broken.

A useful alternative is to store your valuables away in a specialised storage centre (if available in your city). They offer greater convenience and can help you to declutter even more of your property. While this will increase your delivery costs, it will add greater peace of mind for you and more space for your guests.

For your peace of mind, make an inventory of all valuable items, store and lock them away in a safe place. Finally, protect the area with small labels of special tamper-evident tape. If removed, these labels cannot be put back as they will show "tampered with" or "void" or "opened" so that you can immediately tell that someone has tampered with it. It is important to make your guests aware of these areas and explain that a financial compensation may be paid if they remove the tape from off –bound areas.

Arrival info pack

Together with the instructions manual, you should attach a list containing the number of towels, the linen and the keys you expect to find at check-out (to be signed by the guest at check-in), a tourist map of the city, a list with current events taking place and a pre-printed feedback form (very important for building a solid reputation and for getting feedback about the service you provide).

Cleaning the property before the arrival

The cleanliness level is of paramount significance to the rental process and this shouldn't be taken lightly. Even though, in general, people don't expect deep cleaning services where curtains, walls and carpets are washed and professionally cleaned, the cleaning process should still follow the hotel standards of quality.

The bathrooms must be free of lime scale or hair and all windows and mirrors must be left grease and smear free. In the kitchen, the oven and fridge must both be cleaned very carefully and the fridge must be emptied for the guests. All other kitchen equipment must be cleaned so that there is no grease build-up or crumbs anywhere. Of equal importance, wash up all crockery, cutlery, glassware and all pots and pans and arrange them neatly in their drawers. It is good practice to also leave plenty of tea towels for your guests.

All rooms in the house must be vacuumed and dusted everywhere. Pay special attention to corners, skirting boards, window sills, wall frames and anything that can hold dust.

Useful labels with brief instructions

It is another good idea to place small labels with instructions in places where you feel that a quick reference may help. I have used labels for boilers (quick setup instructions), kitchen drawers (with the contents), to mark off-limits areas, or even in the lobby (to show where your mail correspondence should be stored).

This is entirely up to you and although not essential, it is a nice touch for someone who doesn't know your property.

Welcome gifts and compliment slips

You can always add a touch of class with a bottle of wine and a box of chocolates waiting for your guests on the table. Also, handwritten welcome notes create a very strong impression in much the same way as animals made from towels cause excitement among children. Flowers, cheese plates and the most recent copies of fashion, design and local life magazines are always a great treat for everyone.

Chapter checklist

- ✓ Check all access keys and alarm setup instructions. Ensure all locks function very well
- ✓ Put together the property instructions manual
- ✓ Research brand names, quality and the prices for the items used for the property setup
- ✓ Source linen, towels, kitchenware and welcome packs and make arrangements to put away your own sets in a safe place outside of the reach of your guests
- ✓ Setup your TV, internet and audio-video equipment. Check batteries, connections and manuals
- ✓ Store away valuable items and set off-bounds areas
- ✓ Learn how to make up beds according to hotel standards (there are many instructional videos available online)
- ✓ Find specialised storage companies if you decide to store your valuables away and there isn't enough space in your house for this.

12 The arrival process

When both marketing and pre-arrival are done properly, the arrival process should be a very pleasant experience for you and your guests. The process shouldn't take more than 15-30 minutes in most cases and a complete check-in should look like this:

- Ask the lead guest to show you a photo ID and compare it with the booking records
- Compare the signature on the ID with the signature on the agreement (take a photo with both together for future reference)
- Identify all guests in the party and check to see if they are included in the rental agreement
- Go around the house with your guests and explain access, keys, alarms (where applicable), heating and hot water controls (boilers, digital panels), TV and internet access and use, rubbish collection and the local attractions
- Mention the current damages and leave a copy of the inventory with the lead guest. Ask for confirmation and amendments to be sent to you within 24 hours as that will be used for reference in case of disputes
- Explain again your policies for parties, smoking, pets and noise
- Locate and show all off-limits tamper-evident taped areas
- Introduce the info pack. Explain the property manual, emergency contacts and procedures

- Arrange the check-out details such as when and where you will meet to return keys
- Leave the feedback form with the guest and invite them to fill it in before departure
- Ask the lead guest to acknowledge receipt and to sign for the keys, linen and towels (and take this with you)
- Test all access keys and the alarm, ask your guests to familiarise themselves with the locking and unlocking process and ensure that outside gates, concierge desks or entrance codes/fobs are mentioned if applicable
- Confirm the contact telephone numbers you will be using to contact guests if needed

Even though it may look like a complex process, once it has been done a couple of times, it becomes second nature and feels more like a welcome guidance for friends. All the steps mentioned are very important and while the order is not important, you must nevertheless cover all topics.

If this process is outsourced to an agency, you must verify what the standard procedure is and check to see if the essential points below are part of the process. You should expect a high level of professionalism if an agency's meet and greet people take over the task. Ask about grooming standards, skillset and background.

Chapter checklist

- ✓ Pay special attention when you compare signatures on the ID and the rental agreement
- ✓ Never forget to ask your guests to test the access keys and alarms
- ✓ Ensure that they know how to operate the heating and all equipment in the property
- ✓ Check that your guests know who to call in case of emergency
- ✓ Ask the guests to sign for keys, linen and towels
- ✓ Confirm the contact method and numbers if you need to get in touch with the guests during their stay

13 During the stay

Once your guests have arrived and are in-situ, your role is to be reachable for emergencies and support. In my experience, the first two days are the busiest when it comes to support requests. This is the time when people "discover" the house and have trouble pushing switches, turning equipment on and off, unlocking doors or setting up alarms.

The majority of these requests will be easily managed remotely and unless you have a major leak, faulty boiler or jammed lock, the chances are you won't be required to attend or to send a third party support team.

If you leave the city, it is essential to arrange emergency and guest services support in your absence. Later in the chapter we will list the potential areas of concern where your help will be needed urgently.

It is good practice to give your guests a courtesy call the day after arrival to enquire about their first impressions, whether there is anything you can help them with and if the inventory you have left at check-in is accurate. This courtesy call gives you the perfect opportunity to get first hand feedback and to clear all hiccups which may occur. Guests are in general very happy to offer advice and feedback so do not feel afraid of asking, as this is the most valuable and transparent source you have. Much in the same way as the next day calls, you must call your guests two days before departure to arrange for keys pickup on the departure day.

Now, 'what can go wrong?' you may ask. We have looked at this in a previous chapter where we discussed managing risk. There is no simple answer to this and it usually depends on the reliability of the equipment, the cultural differences and the all-important expectations you set during the marketing stage.

If you know that your shower equipment has a sophisticated, last generation water spraying system then you better make sure that you explain to your guests how to operate it, otherwise the chances are that you will receive a call in the middle of the night.

Similarly, if the culture requires them to shower three times a day and you have six people in-situ, this means that your boiler and water tank (where available) will be under heavy pressure for the entire duration of the stay. If the capacity of the water tank is designed to serve only three people showering or bathing once a day, you may receive complaints if the boiler cannot keep up and the water is not hot enough every time it is needed.

When we go into the expectations realm, things can get even more random. US and Australian travellers, for instance, tend to expect very large beds as standard, while Middle Eastern parties are used to big rooms and often with high ceilings. In many countries, dishwashers and washer-dryers are installed as standard so make sure you manage expectations carefully and list your equipment at the booking stage.

Emergency support

You may be required to attend and offer support in case of water leaks, broken windows, jammed locks, alarms going off, blocked toilets and sinks, faulty boilers, TVs, fridges, lights or even broken beds.

When this happens, support is needed immediately, and I highly recommend that you maintain a list of emergency support providers for the following services:

- Locksmiths
- Plumbers
- Carpenters
- Boiler specialists
- Electricians
- Window glaziers
- Emergency carpet and sofa cleaners
- Your security alarm provider

The help of a friend or family member is always a plus but be aware that you will need to issue invoices and receipts for all damage work if you expect your guests to pay for anything.

Concierge services and extra cleans

This type of request is usually more difficult to deal with if you manage your property alone and you are out of town for the duration of the stay. If you have someone to help, then extra cleaning provides the ideal opportunity to keep your property in top shape and to actually keep an eye on how careful (or not) your guests are with your house. Booking tickets to events in town, arranging car transfers or sending flowers are highly valued concierge services but again, be very careful when offering them as they come with a host of expectations, responsibilities and processes to be managed. This is usually the domain of agency services and it is better to stay away from it than over-promise and under-deliver.

Chapter checklist

- ✓ Set reminders for arrival and departure courtesy calls in your diary
- ✓ Research and enrol the help of all specialists listed above (family and friends are all welcome)
- ✓ Review your emergency attendance and resolution times and ensure that guests are aware of them
- ✓ Purchase enough linen and towel sets to accommodate any extra clean and linen change you offer
- ✓ Think about what concierge services you want to offer and plan accordingly

14 The departure and post-stay setup

Owing to the fact that properties are scattered around the city, the departure process may not be similar to the ones we are all used to from the hotel industry. There is no front desk to deal with enquiries, arrivals or departures and that is why you need to agree in advance with your guests what will happen on the day of departure.

If you don't need to meet your guests on departure, simply ask them to do a quick check around the house to lock windows and doors, turn off water, gas and lights and then leave and place the keys in a secure place which you will have prepared in advance. In some countries, entrance doors have letterbox frames so that keys can be posted through the box. In other countries your guests can leave the keys in the mailbox which should be locked at all times anyway.

However, if you want send someone to meet your guests or you want to do it in person, make sure that you agree a time for this. Always be punctual because on the day of departure guests have trains or planes to catch and they have a very tight schedule.

Even if you don't meet your guests at check-out, it is imperative that you either visit the property yourself or send someone to do this as soon as possible, ideally the same day. This is an essential security process and you have to make sure that the following areas are checked:

- All windows and doors are shut and locked

- The gas (kitchen equipment, fireplace), water and lights are turned off

- The alarm (where available) is active

- There are no major damages or ongoing maintenance issues

- You receive all sets of keys that you have given to your guests on arrival

- The rubbish is not left in an unauthorised place outside the property

Once the property is secure and safe, you can schedule the post-stay clean, inventory and the preparation for your return for a later date.

If the clean and inventory are not done immediately, it is important to let your guests know when this will happen because you cannot release the damage cover guarantee until you inspect the property and put together a new inventory. As you would expect, guests will become impatient if they have to wait too long for you to release the amount you are holding, so the sooner you can complete the process, the better it is for everyone.

Post-stay setup

In order to return the property to its initial state you will have to follow the steps below as soon as you can:

- Post-stay inventory to identify any new damage or missing items

- Beds setup. Strip the beds and make them up with your own linen (or new sets if there is a new booking coming up)

- Inspect the off-bound areas and remove tamper-evident tape (keep if there is a new booking coming up)

- Clean the property and retrieve what's left from the welcome packs (look for the feedback form)

- Check that the kitchen and the audio-video equipment are functional

- Send all linen and towel sets to laundry (or launder in-house although I recommend against for health and safety reasons)

Once the post-stay inspection and clean are complete, you must contact your guests and inform about any amounts you will be taking from the damage cover guarantee.

If there are damages, it is common courtesy to send a brief message to your guests to inform them that damages have been found and that you will be back with details as soon as you have them. Once the repairs and replacement are complete you must contact the guest with a final update. Be very specific, explain the situation, refer to the signed arrival inventory and attach invoices for all repairs or replaced items.

Chapter checklist

- ✓ Decide if you want to meet your guests on departure or not
- ✓ Arrange the details for same day inspections to take place if guests are not met on departure
- ✓ Prepare an email template to be sent to the guests with the next steps for inventory dates and damage cover guarantee release
- ✓ Conduct the post-stay setup procedure

✓ In case of damages, follow up for repairs or replacement and confirm with the guests the final amount in writing.

15 Damages - what to expect and how to deal with them

This is one of the most discussed topics and it is easy to understand the reasons. Whenever something bad happens, someone must pay to make things right and, as the saying goes, *the devil is in the details*. In theory, everything is clearly cut and as long as you identify the damage and the guest agrees with the check-in inventory everything is alright. In practice though, no matter how careful you are there will be situations when the damage is in a grey area or the balance between revenue, reputation and keeping the guest happy will favour a different path.

The list below describes the most common risk areas and what to do in case there is damage:

Carpets and flooring

These are the most vulnerable because they can be easily stained, soiled, dented or ripped. Even careful guests may drop a glass of wine on your carpet or put dents in your wooden floors when wearing shoes with high heels. If you have light coloured carpets, make sure that you ask your guests to take their shoes off when inside the house. Also, try to explain that eating and drinking in bedrooms and areas other than the kitchen or dining room is not permitted. I recommend that you encourage your guests to report all incidents immediately.

In most incidents where carpets are stained, the sooner you attend, the more efficient the cleaning process is. Advise your guests to refrain from trying to clean the stain and to just use paper or a sponge to dry up the area. This is because every substance affects different materials in different ways and without professional training there is the risk of causing even more damage.

Wooden floors are vulnerable to indentations (shoes with high heels), marks from suitcases or the impact caused when dropping, pulling or pushing heavy or sharp objects. When this happens there isn't much you can do and specialist advice and support is needed. The cost for repairs can vary greatly depending on the quality of the materials used but in general it is considered an expensive operation.

Tiled floors can be equally expensive to fix and the usual damage is a cracked or scratched tile. While they can be far more resistant than natural wood, when damaged, the repairs can cost a lot because the operation may involve the removal of other adjacent tiles.

If you don't feel comfortable with the level of risk then it is good practice to cover the area with a standard carpet for the duration of your rental.

Sofas, armchairs and dining chairs

People like to have a snack while watching TV and your guests won't be different. Children love to roam the place holding a cake or ice cream in their hand and more often than not the food will end up on your brand new sofa. Dining chairs are in the same risk group and there isn't much you can do about it.

Much like the incidents with carpets, stains on fabric can be very difficult or even impossible to remove and that is why you need to remind your guests to report all incidents as soon as possible.

If you have expensive sofas and armchairs, you should definitely look to cover them with decorative throws which can protect them and also add a beautiful note to the room.

However, be prepared to have to deal with damage so keep records of the manufacturer's care instructions for all upholstered pieces of furniture.

In case of cuts or tears it is best to seek specialist advice and the cost is almost invariably higher then cleaning stains.

Kitchen and kitchenware

The kitchen is the place where people "play with fire" as they say. Objects can be burned, cut, scratched, stained and everything in between. It is therefore critical to use a two-pronged approach to avoiding damages. On the one hand, you must provide your guests with enough protective items like pads, supports, tea towels and table mats and on the other hand, you should make your guests aware if worktops are made from easily stainable materials like marble, Corian or wood for example.

Modern glass hobs are another area where cracks and burned grease can damage the material and careful use is recommended.

The kettles, toasters and microwave ovens are not so vulnerable unless dropped on the floor by accident.

The crockery and glassware are again vulnerable to cracks and chips and there isn't much to do to protect them other than to place them in easily accessible cabinets. Even though they are vulnerable, this shouldn't have a big impact on your cost profile because you will use standard quality sets, therefore replacing an item should be quite inexpensive.

Decorative objects

The rule of thumb is that the more clutter you have in your house, the more likely it is to have to deal with damaged lamps, vases, photo frames and similar decorative items. Usually, these will be scratched, chipped, cracked or broken and the most likely solution will be to replace them. That is why it is important to keep purchase receipts so that you can refer to the correct price when charging for a replacement.

As mentioned in a previous chapter, you must store away all valuable and irreplaceable objects otherwise the implications will go beyond their monetary value.

Walls and doors

Walls and doors are usually scuffed and the suspects are the suitcases and travel bags guests carry with them. Occasionally, there may be colour pen marks on the lower half of the walls as children appear to prefer this support for their creative activities. When this happens, the first trick in the book is to use special cleaning sponges available from all major DIY stores. A word of caution though - depending on how dirty and dated the entire wall is, there is a risk of cleaning the scuff and creating a big discolouration right in the middle of the wall. Just imagine how your clean area will look like if the rest of the wall has a grey shade.

Doors are more resistant in general and it takes much more to damage them. Lacquered surfaces can suffer however if pushed with sharp objects.

TV and audio-video equipment

All equipment can be scratched, broken or electrically damaged when affected by spilled liquids. If this happens, there isn't much you can do to polish the surface or repair the circuit boards. For scratches and chips, you can ask for compensation whereas for damages due to spilled liquids - if the device has stopped working, you can charge for replacing the unit. Lost remote controls are the most frequent type of damages in this category, but usually they are easily replaced and in the most cases the cost is not prohibitive.

Smoking, fumigations and pets

These are all quite damaging as the smell and pet hair go everywhere. Smoking and fumigating for religious purposes will impregnate curtains, carpets, walls and all soft fabrics with a persistent odour. Pet hair will stick to all upholstered surfaces and the fluffier a carpet is, the more difficult and lengthy the cleaning process becomes.

If the smoking and/or fumigation were a one-off incident, you can hope that the smell will clear completely within one week. However, if this was done constantly for the duration of the stay then you have to consider arranging for the property to be professionally deep cleaned. This involves washing the carpets, curtains and walls as well as a very thorough dust and dirt removal. If needed, you can even place a special ozone machine inside to clean up the air and remove the smell of smoke, incense or various aromatic oils used in fumigations.

Pet hairs usually require special vacuum cleaners equipped with water extraction systems. These are very effective on carpets but cannot be used on sofas or armchairs, so the process can still be tedious and have varying degrees of success.

In any case, the charges you will want to recover are higher than a normal clean and the process may take more than a day, which should be added to the final bill as a lost opportunity cost.

General note about replacement value

For all items which need to be replaced, the compensation value is usually calculated using depreciation tables. While the process is not very complicated, you certainly need to do some research to find out the price of the item when new, the expected useful life and this will give the yearly depreciation rate (linear depreciation).

For example, a sofa priced at $500 when new and with an expected useful life of 10 years will depreciate at a rate of $50 per year. If you had it for two years and then you needed to replace it as the damage cannot be repaired -while the legislation may vary from country to country, in general the maximum you will be able to claim is the value left, which in our case is $400. For this to happen though, you will need to show purchase receipts and this may be difficult for older items.

Chapter checklist

- ✓ Take a tour of the house and identify the most valuable and vulnerable objects
- ✓ Ensure that you protect sofas and armchairs with throws, wooden floors with decorative carpets and that you store away all valuable and irreplaceable objects
- ✓ Get into the habit of making your guests aware of the vulnerable areas
- ✓ Put together a folder with purchase receipts for all fittings at risk
- ✓ Find depreciation tables for all decorative objects available to your guests as well as for the kitchen and audio-video equipment

16 Social media and your online reputation

The short term rental industry thrives online and I can say with a high degree of certainty that social media is the most influential medium for building your reputation. Your guests will form opinions and share them with the online community almost in real time. The commentaries will be a mixture of expectations and actual experiences and you should keep a careful eye on them. If you work with agencies, you should read the reviews as often as you can and aim to add your views every time. No matter how negative they may be, in reality nothing is more damaging than the absence of any reaction from the host.

Your replies must stay true to the facts, be objective, brief, offer an equitable solution if needed and reaffirm your availability for support if required. When putting together a response, you have to communicate your views not only with your previous guest but with all future guests who will be interested in your property. This aspect is essential because your potential guests will certainly research your online reputation and read your comments too. A quick, informed and objective position accompanied by clear explanations and offer for assistance is a very positive signal for all prospective guests. Mistakes happen but the way we react to them is what matters the most.

When you start out, each review matters enormously because the rankings are very sensitive to variations in the numbers of stars, points, weight or whichever ranking is used. The more reviews you have, the less influential each individual one becomes but it is more and more difficult to improve the overall score of your property. Consistency is the key element and this can be achieved by managing expectations and by delivering the expected product and service.

TripAdvisor®, Facebook® and Twitter® are the most obvious channels but equally important are the agencies' websites, travel forums and online travel agencies. Depending on your chosen distribution channels you will have to monitor them actively and be ready to contribute your views if required.

It is of utmost importance to try to obtain direct feedback from your guests during and after their stay and to ask permission to use their positive comments online. Real reviews help you to build trust and to balance the negative comments (if any).

17 Emotional commitment

I hope that you are now much more comfortable with the idea of renting out your house. As you can see, there is a lot going on behind the scenes and if you want to have a safe and profitable experience you must adhere to the processes outlined in this book.

If you remember, in the introduction I wrote about the emotional commitment needed for this business and I want to return to this topic in the final chapter. The prospect of easy money is a powerful magnet for everyone and property owners are ideally positioned to take advantage of this new business model.

Having said that, the prospect of having strangers sleeping in your beds, using your kitchen equipment, roaming the place and searching every corner of your house is genuinely daunting. After discussing this subject with many people involved in the business, I put together an objective mini-guide to gauge how likely you are to enjoy the experience. The analysis method below helps the decision making process and it is particularly useful when dealing with emotionally-charged decisions:

- *How significant is the potential profit in the economy of your family?*
  The higher the number the more attractive the proposition becomes. Couple this with certain circumstances when money is indeed a life saver and this can be a great incentive.

- *Have you celebrated any significant family events in this house like births, weddings and the like?*

We attach emotionally to significant events in our life and the place where these events take place becomes very special. The more special it is, the less inclined we are to share it with strangers.

- *How long have you lived in the house?*

Memories and habits tend to be strong barriers to short term rentals and the longer you live at the address, the stronger the bonds become.

- *How many people live with you and how likely are they to share your short term rental plans?*

Plans are just plans, ideas waiting for acceptance, validation and common effort. If you have a large family living at the house, sometimes it takes a lot of convincing to do before they all agree to the idea of having people sleeping in their beds and using their things..

- *Is there anyone else in your neighbourhood already renting their place out short term?*

Peer pressure is a reality and the more people that enter the industry; the easier it is for others to join in. If you live in an exclusive, gated community governed by a board of owners and no one rents their flat out short term, it may be daunting to start the ball rolling.

- *Do you have friends or other family members already renting out their properties?*

  As above, if other family members or friends rent their properties out, it is easier to jump in and get advice and support from them.

- *What is the cultural consensus about short term rentals in your local community and city?*

  This is a very new business model and there is still resistance at various levels. Both sides have strong arguments and unless you have an equally strong plan, it may be daunting to start out in a place where people haven't adopted the sharing economy yet.

- *Do you have expensive fittings like designer chairs, tables or sofas?*

  Our house is our temple and it is normal to invest in it constantly. The more you invest and create and the higher the price paid for this, the less likely you are to take the risk and give unsupervised access to your house to strangers.

- *Have you ever entertained at your place? Do you throw parties and have people sleeping over at your house?*

  If your lifestyle is defined by parties, entertainment, sleepovers, travelling and sharing then this business should be a natural addition to your habitat. However, if you lead a quiet life and receive only a relatively small group of people for dinners and celebrations then the prospect of having strangers in your house may be difficult to contemplate.

As you can see from this excursion into the emotional element of renting out your place, we are the measure of all things. It is up to us to know where our priorities are and to balance the above emotional levers according to the big picture.

Short term rentals have the potential of adding tremendous value to the life of many people who enjoy living like a local, and *you* are central to this business. Whether you will want to go it alone or enlist the help of professional agencies, you can rest assured that when done correctly, this is a safe and profitable proposition for all parties involved.

18 About the author

The author has spent the last 20 years in the hospitality industry and is still an active player in the short term and holiday rental market in London, UK. He is at the forefront of the short term rental revolution and has contributed to the creation of the fundamental building blocks of service delivery in this field.

The author has held key positions with many of the best hotel chains in the world and thanks to this rich professional experience he is uniquely positioned to understand the needs and expectations of all stakeholders.

For his advisory projects, the author has put together highly relevant development and operational strategies which are equally useful to complete beginners and to more experienced operators. He lives in London with his wife and their three children.

For new projects or enquiries related to the topics discussed in this book you can contact us at enquiries@micasasucasa-consulting.com and we will be in touch with more details.

Printed in Great Britain
by Amazon